World, Composed

poems by

Jessica Reed

Finishing Line Press
Georgetown, Kentucky

To: Jessica
From: Sara Rosnick

World, Composed

In memory of Tom Andrews, mentor and friend (1961-2001)

Two thousand years ago, the Roman poet Lucretius wrote the first poem about atoms. Long before there was experimental evidence that atoms were real, Lucretius described in *De Rerum Natura* (*On the Nature of Things*), a universe of invisible, indivisible, particles that make up our world. Even in his time, atoms were strange: as Italo Calvino would later write, "The idea of the world as composed of weightless atoms is striking: we know the weight of things so well." Maybe not weightless, but without the heft of the world we pull ourselves through. Ours is a time when we have seen inside atoms; we know they defy common sense. The atomists insisted on a void; without emptiness, atoms would have no room to move and nothing would ever happen. But we have since learned that the emptiest of spaces is teeming with fields. Spacetime is physical. The words of Niels Bohr, who gave us our planetary picture of the atom (a mere cartoon of the real object), guide this project: "...when it comes to atoms, language can be used only as in poetry."

ACKNOWLEDGMENTS

Thanks to the editors of the journals where the following poems appeared, sometimes in
different forms:

Conjunctions: "I Dreamt I Saw an Atom Bare," "Enter: Matter," "Matter, Resistance,"
"Measure," "Little Room in the Mind," "Exotic Atoms and the Visible World"
Web Conjunctions: "*Atomos*, World Composed: A Canonical Dialogue with Lucretius"
Crazyhorse: "Light, a Disturbance," "Entropy"
Bellingham Review: "General Relativity: A Natural History of Motion," "The Unreasonable
Effectiveness of Language in Special Relativity"
Colorado Review: "Space without Objects"
New American Writing: "Worldlines, or Place as Literal"
North American Review: "Wake: World, Arrived"
Waxwing: "Orbiting the Nucleus"
Spiral Orb: "Atom, Cathedral," "Particle"
Isotope: A Journal of Literary Science and Nature Writing: "Higgs Field, Dancer Beauty"
The Fourth River: "Light, Pinned and Singing," "A Model for the Destruction of Hard
Things," "For the Troubled Mathematician Who Confronted Remote Infinities," "Late
Summer in Indiana, as the Earth Passes Once Again Through a Band of Comet Debris"
Tinderbox Poetry Journal: "Red"
Kudzu House Quarterly: "The Persistence of Aether"

I am especially grateful to my husband James Cook, whose love makes my life possible. And
to Emily Koehn, who has patiently read and given feedback for many years, whose poetic
insights and friendship I cherish, and whom I have to thank for encouraging me to finish
this project. With family, I have been profoundly lucky—they are who I am.

Special thanks to Bradford Morrow and Micaela Morrissette, and to Leah Maines at
Finishing Line Press for supporting this chapbook.

Publisher: Leah Maines
Editor: Christen Kincaid
Cover Art: E. L. Trouvelot
Author Photo: Deb Reed
Cover Design: Jessica Reed

Printed in the USA on acid-free paper.
Order online: www.finishinglinepress.com
also available on amazon.com

Author inquiries and mail orders:
Finishing Line Press
P. O. Box 1626
Georgetown, Kentucky 40324

Table of Contents

I Dreamt I Saw an Atom Bare

> *An intellect which at a certain moment would know all forces that set nature in motion, and all positions of all items of which nature is composed, if this intellect were also vast enough ... it would embrace in a single formula the movements of the greatest bodies of the universe and those of the tiniest atom...*
> —Pierre-Simon Laplace

Branches on bare trees in winter. What's left.

No clouds of probable, only the bones of the possible—as if god refused to be mysterious,

just once, at those speeds and those masses. Icicles. Water, held in place.

This, to embrace the movements of the tiniest atom—to be a mind in deepest space,

single formula. Imagine a truly empty jar: first some *thing* in it.

Now, subtract. Sand and root and trickle. I have hundreds of stories to tell. I'd rather

come at them glancing. It's one way to be afraid. Once, god had birds' eyes,

saw every ultraviolet latch and hook, wheel and paddle. Such an intellect

would know every force that set nature in motion, every address of every furnishing, hold

the universe entire. Physics: that we might know what god knows. (We might be god.)

Imagine such a mind—flash of fish turning in light—you *have* such a mind!

And all at once: coitus. Seed in pod, unfurl.

Light, Pinned and Singing

I am finally present. As Virginia said,
My eyes are hard. Years ago now,
in optics lab, my partner's strange
pronunciation of 'frosted glass'.

We were looking at spectra then: glass-
shattered light lines. But I couldn't focus.
Those radiant projections—just as dazzling
as their sources. The glisten of one borrowed

from the other. And elsewhere, gaseous auroras
both southern and strange. They'd been there
the whole time. Facts may not shimmer,
but they are star-like occasions for metaphor. Even

if I have to bend them a little. That *white
celestial thought.* Virginia warned us
all: *the light is fitful.* White beams of winter,
wind compresses snow into hard

barricades. Shakespeare said fires *singe
my white head!* In kitchen sinks and pressure
chambers, we manufacture fourteen shimmering
forms of ice. See, I believed Tom when he said

There is indeed some light in us. We seek
to explain it, lest our own fitful light dissipate,
star-like in its collapse, with each
photon no longer so startlingly distinct.

Enter: Matter

I believe in blue fields:
one hundred thousand hectares of shrimp farms
in Ecuador. Wetlands and salt flats
along the Pacific coast have made room
for cyan rectangles. You can see them

from space. Convinced by brisk and cleaving
order, its contours. And so the atom: idea, quarrel,
and finally. Understand, it was one thing
to sort elements by kind, another entirely
to believe. Mendeleev did not doubt

the solidity of stuff, yet, working with silver,
sulfur and sodium, could not regard
a single silver atom as true. He believed in cold,
crystalline order, but refrained: not Mendeleev—
not anyone—had seen a solitary particular.

But his century turned,
          the atom burst open, and inside: electrons, protons—
                    stable constituents of matter. And it kept bursting,
          inside and further still and held together
                    and immersed within. We threw
                              circus particles at each other, bent
          their paths in charged fields. They collided,
                    decayed, and we examined their debris. Unbound,
          their pieces flung. Photon, neutron, neutrino,
                    gluon, muon, pion … Because we carve.
Let us gather this fugitive matter, name the curious and unfamiliar.

Darwin's Galápagos made possible by naming (*Vampire finch,
Mangrove finch, Green warbler finch*) what divisions
had already happened, island accidents whose names
made the scattered specific. We must believe this:
there are no old or new electrons. We can't follow

one around, pick it out in a crowd. And quarks,
down indistinguishable from down, strange from…
Hidden from sense, these silverfish dart (colorless color,
spin without spin) when we approach. Believe in contours,
in fields of blue, this carving made holy and specific.

3

Atom, Cathedral

> *Make a fist, and if your fist is as big as the nucleus of an atom, then the atom is as big as St Paul's, and if it happens to be a hydrogen atom, then it has a single electron flitting about like a moth in an empty cathedral, now by the dome, now by the altar.*
> —*Tom Stoppard*

Open your mouth, and if
   your mouth is as dark
as an oil slick,
   then the moths in your mouth
will wing against your teeth…

I only want to say one true thing.

   With the moon as reference, a moth
flies straight. Perhaps our false moonlight
strips away optical infinity,
   or its search for nectar undoes it:
ultraviolet light reflected off flowers draws
the nocturnal moth.
     (Either way,
it beats around near candle or lamp
   in confusion, not desire.)

The poet I knew best said, *There are cathedrals
we never see.* So: open your mouth, make
   a fist. This is physics.
To a nameless intellect we pray,
   in that vast moth-filled colonnade.
   Descriptive equations rise like smoke
from an altar. We witness the electronic
   structure of the atom,
     the tangled shapes,
the many geographies of now-by-the-dome,
     assembled here
   in the world's first body.

Orbiting the Nucleus

Swift and far beneath the air, an electron
embodies presence and haste. This leaping
      lepton—a hurricane can't keep pace—is never
      still: pin it down, lose it entirely.
      To know it is careening is to become unsituated:

the clocked electron resides anywhere.
I would have told you about metal blades,
      tiny turbines in gas-filled glass tubes—its discovery—
      but I've been distracted by the return stroke of lightning,
      the speed of light in a diamond, darting

faster than voltage can caper across vitreous tubes.
Imagine shadows of cathode rays moving in perfect straight
      lines across the glass. These same rays' shadows
      bend in the presence of a magnet.
      A century of arcs and curves,

torn swirls and swept tracings bending around, shooting
across, looping around again, paths warping in fields.
      An electron on display in school—Styrofoam
      planet, held by cosmic toothpicks, central
      sun-nucleus of protons, neutrons. Skip

across scales: mammoth, mini. Never mind childhood models,
electrons are more like clouds. Suspend oil drops,
      time their earthly fall—pit gravity against electricity—
      find the electron's mass. Millikan swore
      he had seen it, he could count negative charge

as easily as fingers and toes. The electron's charge exactly
opposite the proton, yet tiniest fraction
      of the proton's size and mass. Those trails will tell you
      almost anything. Though we cannot paint an electron
      red let us see it bare: reserved as its contours, saying
                                nothing.

Matter, Resistance

> *Matter is not what it appears to be. Its most obvious property—*
> *variously called resistance to motion, inertia, or mass—can be*
> *understood more deeply in completely different terms. The mass of*
> *ordinary matter is the embodied energy of more basic building blocks,*
> *themselves lacking mass.*
> —Frank Wilczek

Pomegranate seed, avocado pit:
positioned in space and occupying.

Words about matter are honey,
changing meaning as a mood is altered

by the lighting. Honey, complicating.
Has that thing the word pointed to

changed? Matter, a *not moving.*
Burlap sack of apples I tug. Molasses.

Some thing is in it and making its
resistance. What is that, making

a clock or a hose? A stationary electron,
a proton, a neutron—these have *rest mass.*

One lemon on a countertop, its atoms
teeming with trembling parts. But not

a single photon, a light ray moving
in one direction. Blocks, swimming

and viscous. Study a still life and be still.
We are inside. We swim in it. Life

amasses. It is assembly. Peer inside an object
to its clearest skeleton, dripping

waxy through unempty space. Your body
is wax. You are empty. Your space is full.

Particle

Regarded by physicists as a *material point,*
        nearly hypothetical, real as an egg,
        composed of matter. So little spatial
extent: a place (usually), a thing (barely).

I list the problem's knowns
        and unknowns; write velocity, position, the time
        elapsed. A particle's motion is described.
Should I embroider an address?

A point whose position changes
        in space. Why crumble soil
        between your fingers? Moving
is a function of time. This pointed

fingertip.
        Imagine a tiny dot
        as a ship in the water, in black space
and sailing west to east, always

west to east. One
        cannot chart the motion
        of a body through absolute
space. Instead we define

the positions of bodies
        with respect to one another:
        a lover's body, silly and holy
at once. You there and I here

and *both here* a contradiction.
        "I'm either very small," he said,
        "or I'm nowhere at all." Atoms,
thousands of times smaller

than the smallest
        light waves our eyes
        can see—everything
in an impossible radius.

Little Room in the Mind

Here, the peach tree whose branches bend
under peach weight. Someone is in love
with counting. Someone sorts: *Same, same.*
Yellow is the bullet; yellow is the wave.
Scattering events, decays, bound states—
someone probes less directly *(they're just
too small)*. What is kept there. Someone
finds what is red in it from a breeze.
And then, yellow tearing itself off,
as the seams of these peaches.
Here, such a thing as a massless particle.
Such a thing as an absence which feeds
on matter and light. Mud and cloud obey.

It is a mind that imagines a potential well.
It is a mind that thinks in positions under a curve.
Chambers—cloud and spark and bubble—
chasing a fine yellow thread of evidence. An absence
creates galactic arms. What is apparent: a quickening.
Nautilus driving itself backward—these are the reefs
it encounters. This yellow comes boiling off. A peach
bullet. Peach ballet. You are someone.
Your mind feeds. Red cheeks, there.

Exotic Atoms and the Visible World

Magnify the world's snowy blue-cast
physicality, its forms
       and the blankness beneath.
Here is hydrogen: one electron orbits one proton.
       Made exotic, muon
              displaces electron.
The lone proton will not stay so.

Atoms are strange enough, though, taste
of honeysuckle, vaguely sweet,
       barely there,
the reason you are here.
       Now altered, they embody
              metaphor: an electron is
(like) a pion. Electrons are

unlike cathedrals, dominoes, chess pieces—
Consider the frame
       around the photograph
of a painting of a woman
       posing as something else.
              Massive orbital particles
alter orbits, negative pieces drawn in

toward the center. Some even lie
within the nucleus. Daisies,
       petals the color of snow,
and dark blue Baptisia blossoms
       in series in June's sun, the same colors
              as a bare winter place,
the same divisions of white light.

I only want to say one true thing
(belief in a literal language).
       These atoms we have built,
with their cinching atomic radii,
       parade our questions about those
              whose architecture
we can only probe.

Red

Each day, the electrons grow tired of resembling each other so completely and edge—as a group—toward properties. "Red," one says, but since they are identical, no one knows who said this and they adopt it as their collective stance. "We should like to be red," they say in unison.

And they paint themselves red, but as redness is only a phenomenon of light interacting with atoms, of which electrons are only a part, the electrons realize, one by one or as a group (no one can tell), that they can't be sure whether they have become red at all.

"I was hoping for a change," one says. But since all electrons are identical, it is unclear which of the electrons is most disappointed.

Something keeps escaping them.

They agree that they are relatively light particles and that they often occupy orbitals in atoms. But this is not enough.

"We have charge," one says.

"And spin," another adds.

"I hear the stars can be told from each other," one electron says. "That some are old and some are young, some are larger than others, some are destined for collapse or explosion. That each star has a composition, like a fingerprint."

"This is what we lack," says another electron, whose thoughts are so attuned to the first it is as if they share one mind. "We are not composed of anything but ourselves."

Higgs Field, Dancer Beauty

We peer deeply into matter: fields flirt with impossibly
light particles to breed substance. The Higgs field,
touching tiny quarks, creates mass. Imagine the kind
of interaction that gives rise to mass. Newton, seeking
first principles, dubbed it *a quantity of stuff*. And physics worked.
What is mass? Entombed, tiny bodies quivering, their hushed notes

knocking? These bodies lingered in our chambers.
Traces in every collision invited us to decipher
increasingly minuscule things—near apparitions.
Every whirl a brush with unfathomable dimension.
Thingless things, acting in concert, and we, humbled and alert.
Feynman scribbling in his tiny dime-store address book,

All mass is interaction. His mind caught in pencil—
annotating beside *dancer beauty or call her when
her nose is not red*—that energy is to all mass related,
and all mass was by contact created. Curiously linked
are my hands, stardust, lightning and wind—splendor:
an excess of massy elements here, in me, now.

Overcome by our reach, the limits of our knowing.
I am composed of shifty particles, seemingly empty.
Yet the field, touching tiny things, creates
all that makes me actual. Mysterious interaction—somehow
it is enough to make religion in winter bones, a terrible
beauty. I am awe-struck and unglued.

Atomos, World Composed: A Canonical Dialogue with Lucretius

1
We are obliged to look further...

> Articulate is the night, its moon and branch. Tom and
> I peer into the (locked) Santa Maria sopra Minerva, the
> church where Galileo was tried, imagining
> Latin questions with Italian answers. We are scratching a
> surface.

Everything that makes its way to the light has its material source.

> Seeds of the pomegranate. Truly identical subatomic
> particles—neutrons, protons, and electrons—
> that combine to give atoms their character.

*Roses bloom in early spring, grain grows in summer's heat, grapes on their vines
ripen in season in autumn... the code was there in their seeds.*

> Our elemental amazement: soil, body, star. We are
> obliged to look.

*In Nature things never disappear but are resolved again to the elements that first
made them.*

> Even the shadows of the trees, sinewy and corporeal.
> Doubts about the start of our world.

*If matter just ceased to exist, objects might vanish without need of force to loosen
the ties of their parts.*

> Touch everything that makes its way to the light. The
> hands are chalk. Bodies appear to wink.

*These ephemeral beings are somehow replenished: they cannot—they do not—
disappear into non-being.*

> Uncuttable. Once, the word atom meant. Protons and
> neutrons divide into quarks. Still everything in the world
> made of the same stuff, whether electrons or quarks or
> photons. There is a fundamental sameness. Rock bottom.

Matter, itself everlasting, holds them in its bonds.

> We dust up our eyes with our hands, the two of us
> knocking on that church. Galileo must have stood right

about there. Record of a moment gone. What record but
this.

Things persist until some force appears, and they, disrupted, are reduced to the
elements of which they were first composed.

    Matter, itself: resolved again to the elements, the
    strawberries seem a little painted now.

2
Lest you harbor still some doubts… these minuscule atoms cannot be seen by the
naked eye but rather must be understood from inferences…

    Dust particles inside pollen grains floating in water,
    trembling. Hens peck and scratch the surfaces of the world,
    busy peeling off layers of the real in daily ritual while
    I repeat *atom, atom.* Elements. A drumming. Yet cloud,
    ocean, volcano, hands: all *made of* and invisible.

You cannot see the wind that roils the sea and harries the clouds across the sky's
expanses, but you do not question that it is there.

    Trembling, for no apparent reason. Still, some doubts.

Nothing can touch or be touched, affect or be affected, unless it be possessed of some
kind of physical body.

    Long blades of grass, white asters, and foxtail in the
    field whipped by wind, raised bows busy stringing. You
    do not question it is there.

Winds infuriate lash our face and frame.

    He plays the role of a man in love, and I, a fevered
    madwoman. It's only atoms.

Winds unseen swamp huge ships and rend the clouds and scour the mountain tops
with forest-crackling blasts.

    Winds, and we'll swap roles.

Sightless bodies sweep

    My lover's hand over my mouth. Nothing can touch
    or be touched.

Or think of something that time diminishes—an overhanging rock that the waves of the salt sea gnaw, but you cannot see what is lost at each occasion.

> Never with the naked eye. For you, Lucretius, as for
> Epicurus: an argument.

Nature's workings depend on the actions—and therefore the presence—of bodies that are not seen.

> Scanning tunneling microscopes, bubble and cloud
> chambers, high-energy particle accelerators make your
> case: we can see now.

Things of the world are not clumped together in one solid mass but instead there are also voids or empty spaces.

> Between moon and branch. Something that time
> diminishes.

3

...emptiness that allows for the possible movement of things.

> A long time the desert has sharpened for you, broadening its subject.

Look around at the world. However small a body is, it will have heft and substance...

> One half pound, fused palate. A fist. What was once indivisible.

These things which are primal, no power can quench, for they endure, solid, stolid, unchanged.

> What is light in it, leptos. What is heavy, adros. Allowing for the
> possible movement of things.

The bodies cannot be dissolved, destroyed by blows from without, nor pierced, nor decomposed from within, nor assailed, nor shivered.

> Bare protons, boosted. Their clockwise and anti-clockwise beams
> collide.

Without voids nothing is crushed or split in two, or shattered, or broken.

> The heavy ones—protons and neutrons, made of quarks. The light
> ones—electrons and muons, fundamental.

There are tiny bits at the edge of what our senses perceive and can report: and there at the tiniest point, the smallest possible thing exists, without component parts, but a part of something larger.

> Heft and substance. It is a region of descendings. It is a region of ascendings.

There must be some ultimate smallness, some tiny thing that cannot be further subdivided.

> In the apple-sized universe of 10^{-35} seconds, were we, unconfigured, somehow there?

The extent and the depths of space are so great that not even the quickest lightning bolts can traverse it all...

> Yes, Lucretius, and yet: entanglement, span of the visible universe, the real waters. À l'heure où blanchit la campagne, the smallest possible thing exists.

In other words, the world is standing upon itself.

> ( )

4

This is what happens in air, or the gleaming light of the sun.

> It is only air resistance that prevents raindrops from striking the ground at unsafe speeds.

...to join and attune their individual motions.

> Mercury pools and gathers into its metallic self. Of the world and in it. What Tom might have said. Questions in one language, answers in another.

Atoms are tossed around in the empty void... the busy dance of motes in the air, for such turmoil shows the secret of unseen motion in all matter. This restlessness is what they inherit.

> Or in the gleaming light of the sun. As if blue or smooth or salty. The busy dance of motes in the air. Punctuated. A kind of textured quiet.

...atoms, carried down through the void by their own weight do not proceed in an

absolutely unswerving line...

> One voice, interrupting another. Solid and single. Galileo
> in Latin. Galileo in Italian.

Objects fall through an unresisting void.

> A world exclusive in its metrical fog. Occasion for nature.

5
The mind is delicate, fragile, and made of tiny particles.

> Expressions in volcanic glass. Tom and I struggled. I
> mailed medication to Rome.

*There is also something else, mysterious and nameless, and nothing in the world is
diaphanous as this.*

> Wires pinned to a surface. These are fasteners, holding
> stars together.

*This substance is hidden away in the body's recesses, deep but vital—tiny, scanty
elements that carry the force of our mental powers...*

> Constellations disband; we perceive invisible wires
> stretching. The mind is delicate.

*Think of when there is dust that has settled upon your skin, or chalk perhaps, or
mist at night, or a spider web that you neither see nor feel.*

> Numbers, exceeding the space the world has for them. A tightening of
> the fingers.

...or a feather.

> Once we gave up seeing the substance that clothed
> things, the airy concept beneath.

*Think of mosquitoes' footsteps, they approach where one of those spirit atoms is
lodged and you begin to feel it...*

> Webs of chalk, somewhere past the atmosphere. Our
> contact with the real.

...smaller than atoms of cloud, or smoke. With the mind and spirit in such turmoil,

there is incoherent raving.

Premature, the troubled light in the river. An
unnecessary hypothesis, what slides on a frozen lake. An
atom is lodged and you begin to feel it.

6

*Let us consider the nature of things immortal—absolutely solid and unaffected by
blows, allowing nothing to penetrate them or split them.*

"A screw loose": the fibers of the world tied to my mind.

Do spirits have eyes? Or hands?
How else would they know where they are?

Tremor. A light outside swerves, nothing to penetrate. It is only the ends
of the world's fibers I know.

The void persists forever, because space is unaffected by blows it cannot receive.

The world-stuff, nothing to liken it to. Eyes? Hands?
Sewing white thread into stone and convinced of the
symbolic character of physics.

I mean the entire universe itself, the sum of all things.

This word, *reality*, a caught thing, the very small part of
the world the land is.

With what other part of ourselves do we experience madness?

Lucretius, you console me. There is discipline and
trembling upon the waters.

*And even if we suppose that some kind of awareness does persist, it won't be our
awareness.*

Reality, where fish live so deep they have lights in their
heads.

*In all that endless time with all the motions of matter, try to imagine what the
atoms have done and been.*

Suppose an element common to other consciousnesses,
among the bones.

The atoms danced away from the life that was and then, by chance, some happened again to reassemble...

In this corner, somehow less formal than the others?

Finally, in the dark, you can handle an object and feel the shape and texture that you recognize as the same as what it had in the light.

Symposium of worlds presented to different minds. The world twists and rights itself in each lit mind.

Brightness is much stronger than darkness, more mobile, and made of finer elemental pieces.

Statements made by the bleary-eyed must be true or false.

What we call our shadow is air deprived of light.

Handle an object. Touch its unbearable brightness.

7
We move, and the spot we have left fills up again.

Amplitudes of bronze.

What we took to be our shadow is what persisted and followed us along— but these are a series of shadows, with new rays being blocked and then filling up the space.

Bells of the external world line and unline. And the spot we have left fills up again.

The little puddle there in the street is no more than a finger's depth and yet...

City and sky yawn into it. What persisted.

Delivering not words rather the ghosts of language.

A finger's depth and yet drawn to scale.

8
Consider now the air, which, at every hour, changes itself in numberless ways...

What earthworm and lime have to do with the atomic

purr of the natural world.

Heavy earth, the mud of creation.

What Queen Anne's Lace has to do with the colliding
protons of the natural world.

Ether above the breezes, invulnerable to storms and tempests...

What worn hands and children have to do with the
tera-electron-volts of the natural world.

The ether glides with an unchanging and tranquil sweep on high...

What spinach seeds and manure have to do with the
glued nuclei of the natural world.

Its movement slow and unswerving, like the Black Sea's constant current.

What rotting Brandywine tomatoes have to do with the
matter-antimatter annihilation of the natural world.

*What we know about other parts of nature all of which works in the same way with
the same laws,*

What little bluestem has to do with the electron hum of
the natural world.

not only here on earth but up in the sky...

What goose eggs and the ground after a frost have to do
with the whole fermionic cry of the natural world.

9

A cloud, pregnant with lightning fully formed in its belly is struck by a wind...

Articulate is the moon. Who has spoken to you?

You can sometimes watch them form, the innocuous wisps that collect.

Consider the air, at every hour, changing itself in
numberless ways.

Allow your mind to range widely over all the distant quarters of the universe and remember the sum of things.

Trembling. Pregnant cloud, all that collects.

When an alien sky sets itself in motion, it creeps along like a cloud or a mist corrupting our own skies…

We, unconfigured in the metrical fog. The sum of things.

Other signs: dementia, depression, terror, rage…

Troubling, airy hypothesis. Corrupting our own skies.

And some went out of their minds and could not remember their own names.

Other signs: the world's fibers becoming symbolic.

10
We can hope one day to understand more of what is clearly coherent and rational and true.

Discipline upon the waters. We swim with lights in our
heads.

Sun and moon… their light faint or obstructed so that the unsuspecting world is covered in darkness…

In this chambered pomegranate: dark red theorems.

And it leaves us filled with doubts… the walls of the firmament give way to endless strains of restless motions.

Assembled here in the world's first body.

We learned to maintain the dizzying heights upon which we now find ourselves perched.

Endless strains of restless motions, the unsuspecting
world. Material source.

The Unreasonable Effectiveness of Language in Special Relativity

Parting: from your perspective on the train, from mine
on the platform. I claim your clocks tick slow, are out
of sync with each other. We agree that my clock
struck noon, just not about when my noon happened.
Tongues, spineless, investigate the external world,
or speak silent equations—guesses, formal and
systematic. Here are kettledrums and brass bells
reverberating, but only light can keep up
with the mind. The objects on the tip of my tongue
usher in parts of speech. Crucial pieces: *your, my,
simultaneous, happened, perceive*—the violence

of *event*. Let's try to describe: a flash occurred,
just once. ("There is something seductive about these
quantities that do not change from one reference frame
to the next.") Point, radial lines, sphere. Spectacle,
light spreading, everywhere un-splintered and seamless.
What time in my frame did fireworks ignite? What time
in yours? Dilated—more, elapsed. Language comes in
handy: *earlier, later,* a preposition:
to you, to me. When your clock read 12 noon, my clock
read 12:06. Each, respective. We need our words;
pointing, indispensable. Math, as though lifted.

General Relativity: A Natural History of Motion

Not to be undone, wedded
to which modeled universe, gods
spin prepositions, *into*,

from, between matter, galaxies
that shift red, spreading, each I
the center but no center. This hurtling

in every plausible version of the universe,
insists *I am the one, true thou
shalt not stand still.* Acceleration,

the firmament of stars our only reference,
so that (bird, republic, millions):
every blink loosed on the geometric,

the world's lovers calculating
how to turn and sweep. (Spirit:
matter reduced to thinness. Brittle

skeletons of language, vaporing
in every inertial frame.) Worlds
targeting their own shadows,

technique in that rushing (they stay
and stay). Was there anything
inevitable in it? Laws the same whether

speeding up or slowing (stone,
overlap, recognition) or whether—o so thin!—
at constant speed. Manure, white-capped

and nitrogen-rich, the history it contains.
Each moment lived, a shaving off
of what was possible, the narrowing

of outcomes. Mapped bodies,
shedding our prejudice that coordinates
have an immediate metrical meaning,

calling points and events *primary*, never able
to learn the distance between them.
Spine, whose curvature shaped

by wind. Coupling, the conviction
that her grip and interrupted breath
would become his. The ancient Vietnamese

poet, writing of the Real, asks,
"Who drew this bounded landscape?"
Spacetime, outlines of.

Space without Objects

Instead of thinking of space as an absolute necessity, we can regard it as one of the possible states of the universe, just as ice is one of the possible states of water.
—George Musser

How near or far, how blunt the blow:
       like asking the address, in arrow-rain sheets,
of each drop—as in "where is it now?"

Proximity   a nightmare and a construct.
You are your line in spacetime;
                you are tenseless.
All you have or will encounter. Green glass,

trapped air. Like asking icicles to persist
       in July. To point, here.

Your line *seemed* smaller.

The epistemic circumstance of *will I?*
when your future already
       exists. Extract space from causal

events. Knock over a glass, unsteady

and the water is seeping. Its seeping wakes you
and you claw: this is a world line, grow into.

The Persistence of Aether

We must suppose there is void, or hollow space,

       Or instead drape the world in a grid of white lace,

emptiness that allows for the movement of things.

       inviting rooms upon rooms of furnishings.

Or fill space with substance more rare and subtle than air

       We can never step out—white grids everywhere.

or molded steam, unwound by atomists.

       Still we devise ways to reveal what we are fully immersed

We crave contact. A mistake to believe, yet it holds

       in, to spy on god. Aether whispers in our resolute ears,

in place. Is it aether or its metaphor that persists?

       infer me. We are in it again: adrift and somehow fixed.

We cling, we cannot see this web, impossible to resist.

Light, a Disturbance

> *What our senses perceive as empty space is actually the home of invisible*
> *electric and magnetic fields giving birth to self-reproducing disturbances that*
> *travel at the speed of light. ...these disturbances are what light is.*
> —*Frank Wilczek*

No clouds, as if blue were all the sky could summon.

And in that blue, an infinite sheet of charge moving

parallel to itself. And a piece of field birthed here continues

on its own. Now, one field perpetuates another.

A kind of simplicity attained only when one is asked

to imagine what populates empty space. Can I

introspect? I might collapse, doll whose wooden joints are held

by elastic string. Or radiate pure physicality—I might pursue

until raw with exhaustion. Else I am darkness. Your matter

is an emerging from stirring fields. You are impermanent, made

of lasting pieces. Never empty, yet somehow arranged and shimmering.

Are these disturbances what my life is. Clouds gather.

I am never ready. Such facts become fine and sheer at their edges.

Measure

The sky is the reason you can't remember
how language first fell on your small ears.
The sky will turn white and (ellipses)
            constellation and cloud. The sky hangs
its coat of silver on morning's hook.
The sky is indefinite, preceded by a definite
article. It repeats itself and what you hold,
hope to hold, remember holding, is vapor.

Water at these several points, in this instant
not dissipating. Cloud, constellation of drops,
such accounting possible because we imagine
we stop time, imagine infinitesimal
points. Mind of god,
mind over motion and matter
and space between.
            The sky is vast—
this transparent, infinitely long ruler
with infinitely small divisions will measure.

Worldlines, or Place as Literal

worldline
*a curve in spacetime joining the positions of a particle throughout its
existence.*

A halo: contingent
      the spacetime above
this meadow
           (behind the air?)
    is curved everywhere
        I stand, and everywhere
the hay farmer stood
      "before" me.
World lines of grasses,
      bodies, matter given inertia
   by what fills the room.
         (Beneath the air?)
Meter and thing measured.
      Contour of falling snow crystals
on wilting white
      magnolia blooms. Observers
agree only on an interval—
       not when,
          not where,
    not order of events.

And how to interpret?
      Glove of experience,
bodies leaving
      dimensional trails?
      Bin of worms
and dark dirt: consciousness that inhabits
    this void of my keeping.
What pales.
      Pull on what
        comes near.
I move because there is room.

Wake: World, Arrived

Reality, divided into *light* and *matter*.
A moment travels from the universe's birth.

A massless noun converts into light, then reverses.
This, the moment when the universe begins

to shine. Mother's voice whispering by the crib,
brushing with my first series of particulars.

A probability turns true, tips and flashes
slicing the light into particles it daringly

hails through. Father, teaching me to count.
Cosmic microwave background sharpens

to *oldest light*. Coldest light, barely enough
to move a thermometer above absolute

zero, whose space stretched as it traveled,
whose waves grew longer. And space,

hijacking the afterglow. I spend hours,
13 billion years, floating around like this—

stretched, faint, and quiet. You nod,
a kind of blessed observance. I, a high-flying

balloon, raining into space as matter unties itself
into that moment, searing its refrain on our tiny maps.

For the Troubled Mathematician Who Confronted Remote Infinities

Cantor was depressive, too. Paranoid,
      he believed he heard God's voice reciting theorems—
divine mathematical whispers.
      Here, birds eat, drink, and mate on the wing.
Such aerial existence has a certain disadvantage:
come what may, we all end up
on the ground. But the air has substance.

The spaces between stars are filled
with dust and gas. Large African antelope
can survive indefinitely without drinking. Saw off
      layers of antlers to find the atheism of dry things.

Still (and this explains a few things),
stars coalesce from dust and gas; *God's word*
      is flexible. Cantor had proof.

A Model for the Destruction of Hard Things

A woman studying the fracture properties
of coconuts may insist that nature
    breaks its own structures reluctantly, along fault lines
of hard resin on fibrous interiors.

She might apply that principle to apples,
    animal horns and wood,
profile a pineapple so that she might learn something
about destruction.

You stand alone at the edge of ice, push
    a half-submerged tree branch deeper into a hole.
Your branch a lever, the entire frozen pond reacts:
you recognize, (with iterations!) Mandelbrot sets
forming across its surface. It crackles
loudly beneath you, obeying symmetry,
    brokenness: illusions begin
to thaw as water seeps into lines from below.

Coconuts have nothing to do with ice. Levers
do not determine fault lines. The sound of wood
    splitting has nothing to do with the smell
of a forest in January.
            Wait. Apples just might
have everything to do with a pond in winter. I'm suggesting:
a woman in a lab, chiseling antlers to celebrate
    breaking, has everything to do with you
standing in the cold wood, holding a tree branch.

Late Summer in Indiana, as the Earth Passes Once Again through a Band of Comet Debris

On a Perseid night, each meteor
        spends itself.
Every day, the field asks me for nothing.

August each year I have showered in them—
        fragments of Swift-Tuttle. I did not notice
in December 1992 when the parent comet
was nearest the sun (as I learn it was July 1862,
        and will be August 2126)—
        my whole life in the gaping between.

This summer, we saw weather:
        lightning dispatches from the next world.
Striking because we heard nothing.
        The sky an overturned bowl of gray,
the entire horizon south to east un-vanishing,
streaks of electric light, silver threads
        stitching and unstitching not-us:
storms we could see but were not in.
        You wait your whole life for that kind of view:
the actual, showcasing its branched meanings,
        silenced and caught equivocating.

One has to draw diagrams, slice space
        through orbital planes, to clarify
how another's path knifes through ours.
        It is enough
to inhabit one's orbit, to fix one point in the relative
un-fixed.   The radiant point slides
as we turn on our axis, drifts against
the background stars as we orbit the sun.
        I've become a spectator of the known—
of the observable universe of black-
eyed Susans, milkweed, coneflowers, fireflies
and Queen Anne's Lace, staring each day,
        each year until I recognize it:
scope, union, and star system sense.

Entropy

And when my light dissipates
from my temporal skin,
        having astonished me
to the bone (my body is the frame),
the physical system described completely,
        laws will remain, and thin air

will be inhabited
by the facts of this configuration
        of atoms in this time particular.
I have fixed my attention
on those fissures
        of the fractured egg shell and not

on time's forward arrow—so should
the lines repair. Cracked here, and here: the calculus
        of where this flawless ovoid is determined
to break, transcending before and after.
Time's pencil keeps me still,
        tracing actual over possible.

But once the lines have been traced,
I will be amazed at what was ever
        possible. Outside,
it is growing cold. And yet
I have astronomy, the sun, time,
        my barren rhyme.

Notes

I Dreamt I Saw an Atom Bare: Pierre-Simon Laplace's remark is from *A Philosophical Essay on Probabilities*.

Light, Pinned and Singing: "[P]inned and singing" is from a line in Bruce Bond's "Pomegranate"; in-text references are to Virginia Woolf and Tom Andrews; "white celestial thought" is from Henry Vaughan.

Enter: Matter: "Because thou prizest things that are/Curious, and unfamiliar…"—Robert Herrick, from "Oberon's Feast"

Atom, Cathedral: "There are cathedrals we never see."—Tom Andrews, "Paul Celan." Tom Stoppard is from *Hapgood*.

Orbiting the Nucleus: With a line from Marianne Moore's "A Grave."

Matter, Resistance: Epigraph from *The Lightness of Being: Mass, Ether, and the Unification of Forces,* Basic Books, 2008.

Exotic Atoms and the Visible World: In conversation with Wallace Stevens.

Higgs Field, Dancer Beauty: "[D]ime-store address book, *All mass is interaction…dancer beauty…call her when her nose is not red*"—James Gleick, *Genius: The Life and Science of Richard Feynman*; "religion in winter bones"— A.R. Ammons, "Gravelly Run," *The Selected Poems, Expanded Edition*; "a terrible beauty is born"—W. B. Yeats, "Easter, 1916."

Atomos: **A Canonical Dialogue with Lucretius**: I read several translations of Lucretius while preparing this manuscript, but the version I kept closest was David Slavitt's. (*De Rerum Natura/The Nature of Things: A Poetic Translation*, University of California Press, 2008.) "The strawberries seem a little painted now"—Wallace Stevens. "Discipline and sadness upon the waters," "fish so deep they have lights in their heads"—Virginia Woolf. "The human understanding is not composed of dry light"—Francis Bacon. "*À l'heure où blanchit la campagne*"—Victor Hugo. I had been reading a lot of Sir Arthur Eddington's "The Nature of the Physical World."

The Unreasonable Effectiveness of Language in Special Relativity: There is a famous philosophical paper by Eugene Wigner called "The Unreasonable Effectiveness of Mathematics in the Natural Sciences".

General Relativity: A Natural History of Motion: "Spirit is matter reduced to thinness. O so thin!"—Emerson. Coordinates have no "immediate metrical meaning"—Einstein. The Vietnamese poet referenced is Hồ Xuân

Huong, from *Spring Essence: The Poetry of Hô Xuân Huong*, John Balaban (Editor).

The Persistence of Aether: Frank Wilczek referred to the "persistence of ether" in *The Lightness of Being: Mass, Ether, and the Unification of Forces*. The concept of an ether, or some variation of it, has stubbornly reinserted itself into our theories of nature for as long as we've been debating matter and empty space. The latest incarnation is the Higgs field, in which we are immersed and by which particles obtain their mass. Some recommend we think of the viscosity of molasses to understand how the Higgs field imparts mass to particles traveling through it. But imagining this is tricky: the Higgs field seems like an airier, somehow more transparent version of the ether (a supposed medium light waves traveled through) that was famously experimentally discarded by Michelson and Morley in 1887. The vacuum of empty space keeps filling up with friction and drag.
Newton described the aether as "more rare and subtle than air." Some inspiration from John Donne's "At the round earth's imagined corners (Holy Sonnet 7)." "Weave a layer of fine silk gauze and mold steam out of a few red-glowing clouds" is from Wen I-To's "Dead Water," translated by Arthur Sze.

Light, A Disturbance: Wilczek epigraph from *The Lightness of Being: Mass, Ether, and the Unification of Forces*. "If you don't shine you are darkness."—Charles Wright. "Knowledge becomes finer and lighter only at the outer edges..."—Maurice Blanchot.

Wake: World, Arrived: "The division of reality into light and matter seemed self-evident."—Frank Wilczek, *The Lightness of Being: Mass, Ether, and the Unification of Forces*

For the Troubled Mathematician Who Confronted Remote Infinities: Georg Cantor (1845-1918), whose work implied "an infinity of infinities."

Entropy: Some phrases borrowed from Shakespeare's Sonnets XIV, XVI, XXIV.

A general note about Lucretius: I was informed by the scholarship of David Sedley, especially *Lucretius and the Transformation of Greek Wisdom* (Cambridge University Press, 1998). I also used *The Cambridge Companion to Lucretius*, edited by Stuart Gillespie and Philip Hardie (Cambridge University Press, 2007). I greatly benefited from the notes in Ronald Melville's verse translation (*On the Nature of the Universe*, Oxford, 1997).

Jessica Reed has a MFA in Poetry and a BS in Physics, both from Purdue University. Her poetry and non-fiction has appeared in *Conjunctions; North American Review; Crazyhorse; Colorado Review; Bellingham Review; Isotope: A Journal of Literary Nature and Science Writing;* and elsewhere. She taught at Scottsdale Community College in Arizona and for the Johns Hopkins Center for Talented Youth, where she designed special writing courses, such as "Writing Workshop: Where Art Meets Science." She has taught science-themed poetry at a summer program for female high school students in Dammam, Saudi Arabia and a co-ed program in Beijing, China for the Center for Excellence in Education. She teaches a year-long seminar at Butler University called "Physics and the Arts." She lives in rural Indiana with her husband and chickens.

CPSIA information can be obtained
at www.ICGtesting.com
Printed in the USA
LVOW03s1044290318
571613LV00001B/38/P